Contemporary Scenes
for
Young Actors

Douglas M. Parker

A Beat by Beat Book
www.bbbpress.com

Published by Beat by Beat Press
www.bbbpress.com
Copyright © 2016 by Douglas M. Parker

Manufactured in the United States of America

ISBN-13: 978-0692770429
ISBN-10: 0692770429

For my nieces and nephews,
who have caused many scenes
of their own.

TABLE OF CONTENTS

INTRODUCTION

Scenes are the most basic building block of any theatrical work that has a plot. And although not all scenes involve two or more actors, most scenes do. Put two or more actors together onstage and the possibility for almost any situation or emotion instantly comes alive – along with the possibility for every form of human relationship, from equal to unequal to evolving.

With that thought in mind, the thirty-four scenes contained in this book provide young actors with the material to explore a full spectrum of age-appropriate emotions and relationships, ranging from fear to friendship, love to loathing, and cooperation to competition – with moments of sadness, sympathy, silliness, envy, guilt, anger, and almost everything in between.

To help young actors get the most from their experience, the language used in every scene is typical everyday language, rather than the sometimes outdated or highly poetic language that is often found in books of scenes collected from older plays. This emphasis on contemporary language and situations allows the actors to focus directly on the scenes, emotions and characters, without being distracted by unfamiliar words or turns of phrase.

Who is This Book For?

This book was written both for young actors and for the teachers, directors and acting coaches who work with them. More specifically, the material in *Contemporary Scenes for Young Actors* was written to be performed by actors ranging from ages 8-16, with some of the scenes created for actors towards the upper end of that range and some for actors toward the lower end. The scenes are presented in no particular order, allowing every actor the freedom to choose the scenes that best meet with his or her individual tastes, needs, and desire for a challenge.

A Quick Word for Actors

To add flexibility, almost any role in any scene can be played by a male or female actor. Wherever this is not true, the details will be indicated both in the table of contents and in a small note just under the scene's title.

Similarly, while most of the scenes in the book were written for two actors, there are several scenes included that were written for three. The number of actors in each scene is indicated both in the table of contents and directly under scene's title.

When choosing a scene, feel free to explore at random – the individual pieces are presented in no particular order. The goal is simply to find a scene that works with your needs or that challenges your skills. In other words, you may purposely choose *not* to look for the roles or situations that are most like you or that come most easily. You may decide to deliberately choose a scene where the character is absolutely nothing like you or is experiencing an emotion that you are uncomfortable or unfamiliar with.

Finally, once you've chosen a scene, as you prepare, ask yourself a few basic questions: What is the setting? Who is your character? What is your character's relationship to the other character(s) in the scene? And, perhaps most importantly, what is your character feeling and how, when and why do those feelings change over the course of the scene?

Beyond that, just enjoy.

SCENES

PUNISHMENT

(Scene for two people.)

(BAILEY and TAYLOR have been locked in a bedroom as punishment. For the first few lines, BOTH are standing at the locked door, pounding on it and yelling through it.)

BAILEY: Hey!

TAYLOR: Hey!

BAILEY: Let us out!

TAYLOR: Yeah, let us out!

BAILEY: *(To TAYLOR.)* What kind of parents would even do that? Lock their own kids in a bedroom?

TAYLOR: Not very good parents.

BAILEY: Bad parents.

TAYLOR: Terrible parents.

BAILEY: *(Yelling at the door.)* The very worst parents!

TAYLOR: It's not even like we did anything.

BAILEY: Almost nothing.

TAYLOR: Very, very little.

BAILEY: As if a water balloon could even hurt somebody.

TAYLOR: Even if someone threw that water balloon off the roof.

BAILEY: Right? I mean, how high is the roof to begin with?

1

TAYLOR: Maybe thirty feet.

BAILEY: More like twenty.

TAYLOR: Probably ten.

BAILEY: And no one could *drown* from a water balloon.

TAYLOR: Or even two of them.

BAILEY: Not even if they both hit you right in the back of the head.

TAYLOR: It was perfect!

BAILEY: She never saw it coming!

(*BAILEY and TAYLOR laugh.*)

TAYLOR: But that's not what's important.

BAILEY: What's important is that we didn't know that Mom and Dad were standing right on the corner, watching.

TAYLOR: *(Yelling at the door.)* The two worst parents in the world!

BAILEY: Locking their own kids in a bedroom. *(Yelling through the door and rattling the doorknob.)* For two hours! *(To TAYLOR.)* Hey wait a second. This door isn't even locked.

TAYLOR: Really?

BAILEY: Yeah, look. *(BAILEY turns the doorknob, but doesn't open the door.)*

TAYLOR: We could just walk out of here.

BAILEY: We *should* just walk out of here. Except . . .

TAYLOR: I know.

BAILEY: I mean, maybe what we did was the tiniest little bit bad.

TAYLOR: Like ten percent bad.

BAILEY: Or even fifteen percent.

TAYLOR: Yeah. Fifteen percent.

BAILEY: We should stay in here for like fifteen percent of two hours.

TAYLOR: Exactly. Just long enough for them to feel guilty for being so mean to us.

BAILEY: Or we could stay in here for forty percent of two hours and they'd feel even worse.

TAYLOR: I bet at eighty percent they'd feel terrible.

BAILEY: I can't even imagine how they'd feel if we stayed in here for a hundred percent of two hours.

TAYLOR: The worst.

BAILEY: We should do that.

TAYLOR: Teach them a lesson.

BAILEY: Yeah, that'll show them!

TAYLOR: I sure wouldn't want to be them right now.

BAILEY: Me neither.

> *(BAILEY and TAYLOR stand silently for a moment, looking at each other.)*

TAYLOR: How much is left of the two hours?

BAILEY: *(Looking at watch or pulling out phone.)* About an hour and forty-five minutes.

TAYLOR: We'll show them.

BAILEY: Yeah, we'll show them.

> (BAILEY and TAYLOR stand silently for several
> moments, waiting for the time to pass.)

- END SCENE -

GHOSTS

(Scene for two people.)

NOTE: *Although it is stated that the two characters in the scene below are lying in bed, if preferred, the scene can be presented with both actors standing (as though they were lying in bed) or with both actors in chairs (as though lying in bed). Similarly, the sheets mentioned can be real or imaginary.*

(It is the middle of the night. RILEY and KELLY are sleeping in twin beds in the same room. After a moment, RILEY stirs, then opens eyes and sits up.)

RILEY: *(To KELLY.)* What was that?

KELLY: *(Waking up.)* What?

RILEY: That noise.

KELLY: *(Sitting up.)* What noise?

> *(RILEY and KELLY listen for a moment, then are suddenly visibly startled as they hear the noise again.)*

RILEY: That one!

KELLY: Whoa!

RILEY: *(A little frightened.)* It's probably nothing, right?

KELLY: Yeah it's probably…

> *(RILEY and KELLY hear the noise again and jump.)*

BOTH: Whoa!!

KELLY: You should go downstairs and look.

RILEY: No you should.

KELLY: No you should.

>   *(RILEY and KELLY look at each other.)*

RILEY: OK, we both will.

>   *(RILEY and KELLY hear the noise again and react
>   even more startled and frightened.)*

BOTH: WHOA!!!

RILEY: OK, we'll both stay up here.

KELLY: It's probably safer under the covers.

>   *(RILEY and KELLY lie back and pull the their
>   blankets up to their chins.)*

RILEY: Yeah.

KELLY: It's probably even safer all the way under.

RILEY: Yeah. *(RILEY and KELLY go all the way under the covers.)*
   Do you feel safer?

KELLY: *(From under the covers.)* No.

RILEY: Me neither.

>   *(BOTH come out from under the covers.)*

KELLY: You know what? I'm sick of this. I'm sick of being
   scared.

RILEY: Yeah?

KELLY: Yeah. And I'm gonna do something about it. *(Loudly.)*
   Come and get me!

RILEY: What!?!?

KELLY: *(Louder.)* Come and get me!

RILEY: Dude! Be quiet!

KELLY: *(Even louder.)* COME AND GET ME!!!

RILEY: *(Frantic.)* Get her/him! Get her/him!

> *(BOTH look around, waiting. Several moments pass.)*

KELLY: Do you feel safer?

RILEY: No. Do you?

KELLY: *(Uncertainly.)* . . . Sure. Yeah.

RILEY: *(Faking it, but badly.)* Yeah - me too.

KELLY: So we should get some sleep, right?

RILEY: Yeah. Sleep.

KELLY: *(Still sitting up in bed.)* Totally ready for this.

RILEY: *(Still sitting up in bed.)* Yeah. Totally.

KELLY: OK then. *(Faking a yawn.)* G'night. *(Remains sitting up.)*

RILEY: Yeah. *(Faking a yawn.)* G'night. *(Remains sitting up.)*

> *(RILEY and KELLY continue to sit up in bed, staring rigidly ahead, waiting.)*

- END SCENE -

MARATHON

(Scene for two people.)

(BRETT and AVERY enter, jogging. BRETT is several paces ahead of AVERY, jogging comfortably. AVERY is breathing heavily.)

AVERY: Hold up. *(AVERY stops running and bends over, hands on knees, breathing hard.)* Hold up! *(BRETT looks back, but doesn't stop. Louder.)* Hold up!

(BRETT stops running.)

BRETT: What's up?

AVERY: I can't do this.

BRETT: Of course you can.

AVERY: *(Still breathing heavily.)* No. I'm serious. I can't run a marathon.

BRETT: Look, when I did it last year, I didn't think I could finish either.

AVERY: Yeah, but you were wrong. I'm right.

BRETT: You can't stop now! If you don't keep training, you'll never be able to do it.

AVERY: *(AVERY takes a few more deep breaths.)* So? Why would anyone even *want* to run a marathon?

BRETT: Because . . . because it's there.

AVERY: So is the TV.

BRETT: OK. Because not everyone can do it. Because once you do it, you're like part of this secret society of people that . . . get it.

AVERY: Get what? Blisters?

BRETT: I'm serious. You don't run a marathon because it's fun.

AVERY: Yeah. I already figured that out.

BRETT: You run it because it's no fun at all. Because it's so hard that you're not sure if you can do it. But you want to find out.

AVERY: You do know that every time you open your mouth, you make it sound worse, right?

BRETT: Look – this is the deal. If you really do run the whole thing, it hurts. A lot. And it's tiring. And it's long. And it's probably the least fun thing you've ever done in your life.

AVERY: You have got to be the world's worst salesman.

BRETT: But if you make it to the end, there's this, this thing that happens right when you cross the finish line.

AVERY: A thing.

BRETT: Yeah. For one second, but also kind of forever, you're this better version of yourself. You did this thing that you never in a million years thought you could do. That not that many people in the whole world have actually done. And even if you never do it again, you'll always be that person – someone who's run a marathon.

AVERY: I just don't think I can.

BRETT: Look – can you run a hundred yards more?

AVERY: Maybe.

BRETT: So let's do that. We'll run a hundred yards, and then I'll ask you if you can do a hundred more.

AVERY: I think I see where this is going.

BRETT: And then after that, we'll do a hundred more and then a hundred more and then a hundred more.

AVERY: But we'll just start with the first hundred, right?

BRETT: That's it. Just a hundred yards. *(Pointing.)* You can see it. It's right over there.

AVERY: But why do you care?

BRETT: Because last year, when I was crossing the finish line, I was thinking . . . I was thinking that what would have made it even better is if we could have done it together.

AVERY: *(Thinking a moment.)* So, just a hundred yards?

BRETT: Just a hundred.

AVERY: And then maybe *one* hundred more after that.

BRETT: Yeah. Just a hundred and then a hundred more. Ready?

AVERY: Not really.

BRETT: Go!

(BRETT and AVERY exit, jogging.)

- END SCENE -

ORDINARY

(Scene for one Male and one Male or Female.)

> *(Throughout the entire scene, TOM and DREW face out towards the audience – never towards each other. TOM stands to one side of DREW and somewhat behind DREW.)*

DREW: One day about two years ago, my older brother Tom came into my room and said . . .

TOM: Hey, you want to go to the park and play some Frisbee?

DREW: It was a pretty nice out, so I thought, "Why not?"

TOM & DREW: *(Simultaneously.)* It was a completely ordinary day.

DREW: Nothing special about it at all. And we were just laughing and throwing the Frisbee around.

TOM: Go out! Go out! All the way to the end!

> *(DREW takes a step or two back. TOM pantomimes throwing the Frisbee, but not actually towards Drew – out towards the audience.)*

DREW: *(Still looking out towards the audience and pantomiming watching the Frisbee sail towards him/her, then catching it.)* Yeah! *(DREW takes a step or two forward and throws the Frisbee "towards" TOM – but actually out towards the audience – in a high arc.)* High one!

> *(TOM catches the Frisbee, and immediately throws it back to DREW.)*

TOM: Think fast!

DREW: *(Catching the Frisbee.)* Too slow! You're getting old.

TOM: Come here. *(DREW takes a step forward and tosses the Frisbee on the ground. TOM pauses a moment, looking "at" DREW – but, in reality, still facing out towards the audience – and pantomimes ruffling DREW's hair. DREW, still facing forward, smoothes his/her hair back down.)* You know they're shipping me out to Iraq tomorrow, right?

DREW: Yeah, I know.

TOM: That's why I wanted to spend some time with you.

DREW: Yeah?

TOM: To make me even gladder to go.

DREW: *(Laughing.)* Loser. *(To the audience.)* He always talked like that.

TOM: But they already told me how long my tour is and I'll be back three days before your birthday. What do you want?

DREW: Hunh?

TOM: For your birthday. I'll bring you back anything you want. A tank. A battleship. A belt buckle.

DREW: Belt buckle!

TOM: All right, if you're sure. They're giving those tanks away.

DREW: Belt buckle.

TOM: Alright . . . C'mon. Let's throw some more.

> *(TOM and DREW, at first smiling, face the audience silently for several moments as their smiles slowly fade.)*

DREW: *(To audience.)* But Tom wasn't home three days before my birthday. A few weeks before that, two soldiers showed up at the door and gave my mom a letter.

TOM: I'm sorry.

DREW: When my mom showed me the letter, I took it upstairs and I tore it up and I threw it out the window.

TOM: I'm sorry. I'm sorry.

DREW: *(To Tom. Angrily.)* You're a liar!

TOM: I'm sorry I missed your birthday . . . I'm sorry I missed all your birthdays.

DREW: You said you were coming home!

TOM: I'm sorry. I wanted to. More than anything.

DREW: A few weeks later, just exactly on my birthday, a big box showed up at the door with all of Tom's stuff in it. And inside it was a box with a belt buckle in it and a card.

TOM: "To the second or third best brother/sister I'll ever have. Ha ha."

DREW: Cuz I was the only brother/sister he ever had . . . He liked to talk like that.

TOM & DREW: *(Simultaneously.)* I miss you.

DREW: The belt buckle was silver and covered with all these different colored stones. But I never wear it . . . I was so stupid! When he asked what I wanted, I didn't even know that all I wanted was for him to come home. And now all I have is that buckle and that one day in the park. And it was nothing. It was just an ordinary day. But it's the one day with him that I'll never forget.

- END SCENE -

CLUBHOUSE

(Scene for three people.)

(DEVON, DALE and DYLAN are old friends.)

DEVON: OK, I call this meeting of the Thursday Afternoon Super Exclusive Club to order. Does anyone want to second that?

DALE: *(Enthusiastically.)* I will! I will!

DEVON: Awesome. The totally first ever meeting of the Thursday Afternoon Super Exclusive Club is now in session.

DYLAN: *(Raising hand.)* Will there be food?

DEVON: Did you bring any food?

DYLAN: No.

DEVON: Then no, Dylan, there won't be any food.

DYLAN: *(Sulking.)* Fine.

DEVON: Now, the first order of business should be . . .

DALE: *(Cutting DEVON off. Enthusiastically.)* I second that!

DEVON: Thank you, Dale, but I haven't said anything yet. The first order of business should be . . .

DYLAN: *(Cutting DEVON off.)* Why do you get to decide what the first order of business is?

DEVON: Because I'm the president.

DYLAN: No you're not. This is the first meeting. We need to hold elections.

DALE: Is somebody going to bring food next time?

DEVON: OK, Dylan, fine. I nominate myself for president.

DALE: I second that!

DYLAN: OK, then I nominate me for president. *(DYLAN looks at DALE for a moment, waiting.)* Dale?

DALE: What? . . . Oh . . . I second that!

DEVON: *(To DYLAN.)* Dale can't second the nomination of two different people.

DYLAN: Who says?

DEVON; It's the rules.

DYLAN: We don't have any rules yet, 'cuz we haven't voted on anything.

DEVON: Well, we can't vote on anything if we don't have any rules.

DALE: Yeah! No rules, rules!

DYLAN: I move that anyone can second anything they want.

DALE: I second that!

DEVON: Fine. All in favor raise your hand.

> *(DEVON looks at DALE, shakes head, and silently mouths the word, "No." DALE and DYLAN raise their hands.)*

DYLAN: Yes! The motion passes. Anyone can second anything, so we're both running for president.

DEVON: *(Rolling eyes.)* Fine. All in favor of me being president, raise your hand. *(DEVON and DALE raise their hands.)* That's two. Aaand all in favor of Dylan being president? *(DYLAN and DALE raise their hands.)* Dale, you can't vote for two different people.

DALE: Why not?

DEVON: It's the rules.

DALE & DYLAN: *(Together.)* There are no rules!

DEVON: You know what? This is a worthless club. I quit.

DYLAN: Fine! We don't need you anyway. *(DEVON exits.)* I hereby declare myself president of the Thursday Afternoon Super Exclusive Club.

DALE: I move that we should both bring food next week and we have to eat everything we bring.

DYLAN: I second that. *(DALE and DYLAN raise their hands, then quickly look around for any other votes.)* Done.

DALE: Devon is crazy. This is definitely not a worthless club. This club is awesome!

DYLAN: I'll second that.

> *(DALE and DYLAN raise their hands, then quickly look around for any other votes. DALE and DEVON look at each other and smile.)*

DALE: Yeah!

- END SCENE -

SWIM

(Scene for two people.)

(CAMERON and MORGAN are goldfish. Throughout the scene, they are swimming around and around in a circle, inside a fishbowl. They both swim in the same direction. CAMERON is in front.)

CAMERON: *(Passing in front of the audience.)* Ninety-nine.

MORGAN: *(Passing the same spot in front of the audience that Cameron has just passed.)* Ninety-nine.

CAMERON: *(Completing a full circle and passing again in front of the audience.)* One hundred!

MORGAN: *(Passing the same spot in front of the audience that Cameron has just passed.)* One hundred! *(CAMERON and MORGAN continue to swim in the same circle, in the same direction.)* That was fun! What should we do now?

CAMERON: Let's swim in a circle *two* hundred times!

MORGAN: Nah. I'm tired of that game.

CAMERON: Well, what about if I let you swim in front?

MORGAN: I don't know. Do you ever wonder if there's anything more?

CAMERON: More than what?

MORGAN: More than swimming in a circle inside a glass bowl.

CAMERON: I once swam straight across the middle . . . But I didn't like it very much.

MORGAN: No. Something even more.

17

CAMERON: Ohh! You mean eating. I *love* eating. I could eat all day.

MORGAN: Yeah! Me too!

CAMERON: I could just keep eating and eating until . . .

CAMERON & MORGAN: Mmmmmm.

> (CAMERON and MORGAN continue to swim as they blissfully think about eating. After a moment or two, MORGAN snaps out of it.)

MORGAN: But no.

CAMERON: No what?

MORGAN: I don't mean eating.

CAMERON: You're starting to worry me. If you don't mean swimming and you don't mean eating, what *do* you mean?

MORGAN: That's what I'm saying. Something that isn't swimming and isn't eating. It just seems like life is always the same thing over and over. First you pass the chair, then you pass the plant, then you pass the window, then you pass the chair, then you pass the plant, then you pass the window, then you pass the chair, then you pass the plant . . .

CAMERON: *(Cutting MORGAN off.)* I get it. I get it. I mean . . . *(Hesitating.)* There's always the cat.

MORGAN: *(Completely frantic.)* No cat! No cat! We said we're never gonna talk about the cat! We're not talking about the cat!

CAMERON: OK! OK! We won't talk about the . . . the thing.

MORGAN: Don't *do* that.

CAMERON: Sorry. It just slipped out.

MORGAN: Here comes the chair.

CAMERON: *(As they continue around the circle.)* . . . Plant.

MORGAN: *(Continuing farther around the circle.)* . . . Window. It's boring, right?

CAMERON: I don't know. I guess. I never really thought about it.

MORGAN: Wait a second! I have an idea! I don't know if it will work, but it could change everything!

CAMERON: What!?! What?!?!

(*MORGAN swims up next to CAMERON.*)

MORGAN: We could . . . *(MORGAN whispers in CAMERON's ear.)*

CAMERON: Is that even possible?

MORGAN: We should try it!

CAMERON: But . . .

MORGAN: Come on! We should try it! *(MORGAN and CAMERON stop swimming. THEY turn and face each other.)* Ready?

CAMERON: Go!

(*MORGAN and CAMERON turn and start to swim in the opposite direction. CAMERON first.*)

MORGAN: Look! Here comes the chair!

CAMERON: Oh my gosh. This is amazing! And now it's the window!

MORGAN: Look! And *now* it's the plant!

CAMERON: I never dreamed this was possible!

MORGAN: Come on! Let's see what's next!

CAMERON: Yeah! Let's go!

> *(MORGAN and CAMERON continue swimming, as amazed and happy as two goldfish can possibly be.)*

- END SCENE -

MOVING DAY

(Scene for two people.)

(JESS and SKYLER are best friends. JESS is moving away today and they're both unhappy about it.)

SKYLER: So I guess this is it.

JESS: Yeah.

SKYLER: North Dakota, hunh?

JESS: Yeah.

SKYLER: That's like a thousand miles.

JESS: More.

SKYLER: But maybe your parents will let you visit.

JESS: Maybe.

SKYLER: Sometimes.

JESS: Yeah, maybe sometime.

SKYLER: . . . Yeah . . . Remember that time we went camping with your dad?

JESS: Yeah and we saw that snake?

SKYLER: And your dad just *ran*. He climbed all the way up that tree just to get away.

JESS: Yelling down from the top, "Careful kids, I don't want you to get hurt!"

SKYLER: And then he couldn't figure out how to get back down!

(SKYLER and JESS start laughing.)

JESS: Took him like an hour to get down!

SKYLER: And then it turned out it wasn't even a snake!

JESS & SKYLER: *(Still laughing. Together.)* It was a stick!

> *(BOTH laugh for several moments, then stop. JESS and SKYLER look at each other.)*

SKYLER: I don't even know anyone else who likes to go camping.

JESS: When I get to North Dakota, I won't know anyone at all.

SKYLER: I'll call you.

JESS: I know. But it's not the same, is it?

SKYLER: . . . No.

JESS: I'm really gonna miss you.

SKYLER: Yeah.

> *(JESS and SKYLER look at each other, knowing it's probably the last time they'll see each other.)*

JESS: I'll see you around, Skyler.

SKYLER: Yeah. I'll see you around, Jess.

> *(SKYLER exits. JESS stares after SKYLER a moment.)*

JESS: *(Sadly. Not loud enough for SKYLER to hear.)* Good-bye.

- END SCENE -

PARTY

(Scene for two Females.)

(ELLIE and KAYLA are at a party, sitting in a corner and commenting on everyone else.)

ELLIE: Look at Paul.

KAYLA: Seriously.

ELLIE: Can you believe that shirt?

KAYLA: Who wears a shirt like that to a party?

ELLIE: Or anywhere.

KAYLA: It looks like a pajama top.

ELLIE: Who even *wears* pajamas?

KAYLA: Right?

ELLIE: And what is Haley doing?

KAYLA: Is that supposed to be dancing?

ELLIE: Looks more like she's being electrocuted.

KAYLA: Ohmygod, there's that new kid. You know – what's-his-name.

ELLIE: Devon.

KAYLA: Yeah.

ELLIE: Just moved here and he's already captain of the wrestling team.

KAYLA: Like anyone cares.

ELLIE: He probably thinks he's so cool.

KAYLA: Even just thinking that makes him uncool.

ELLIE: Totally.

KAYLA: And he's not nearly as good looking as he probably thinks he is.

ELLIE: Yeah, like anyone cares that he has blond hair.

KAYLA: Or blue eyes.

ELLIE: You couldn't pay me to have blue eyes.

KAYLA: Or dimples.

ELLIE: Yeah, have you seen his dimples?

KAYLA: I'm looking at them right now.

ELLIE: Pathetic.

KAYLA: And the way he dresses.

ELLIE: Like everything always has to be so perfect.

KAYLA: Yeah, like even when he's messy he still looks perfect.

ELLIE: Really sad.

KAYLA: Someone should tell him.

ELLIE: Yeah.

KAYLA: I'm gonna go tell him that, like, we're totally on to him.

ELLIE: Or maybe I will.

KAYLA: What?

ELLIE: I want to be the one to tell him that we're totally on to him.

KAYLA: It's OK. I'll do it.

ELLIE: No. I will.

KAYLA: I was completely not into him before you were not into him.

ELLIE: Uh unhh.

KAYLA: Uh huh.

ELLIE: *(Holding up one hand, ready to play odds or evens.)* OK, odds or evens.

KAYLA: *(Holding up one hand, ready to play.)* Odds.

ELLIE: One, two, three, go! *(ELLIE and KAYLA both put out two fingers.)* I win! *(ELLIE turns and takes a step towards where Devon is standing, then stops short.)* Hey, wait a second. Why is *Megan* talking to Devon?

KAYLA: She would.

ELLIE: I hate the way all the girls around here just keep feeding his ego.

KAYLA: Disgusting.

ELLIE: Hey, do you see what Justin is wearing tonight?

KAYLA: Pathetic.

ELLIE: Someone should tell him.

KAYLA: Right?

(ELLIE and KAYLA look at each other, thinking.)

- END SCENE -

PARTY

(Scene for two Males.)

(EDDIE and KYLE are at a party, sitting in a corner and commenting on everyone else.)

EDDIE: Look at Paul.

KYLE: Seriously.

EDDIE: Can you believe that shirt?

KYLE: Who wears a shirt like that to a party?

EDDIE: Or anywhere.

KYLE: It looks like a pajama top.

EDDIE: Who even *wears* pajamas?

KYLE: Right?

EDDIE: And what is Haley doing?

KYLE: Is that supposed to be dancing?

EDDIE: Looks more like she's being electrocuted.

KYLE: Ohmygod – there's that new girl, what's-her-name.

EDDIE: Rachel.

KYLE: Yeah.

EDDIE: Just moved here and she's already captain of the cheerleading squad.

KYLE: Like anyone cares.

EDDIE: She probably thinks she's so cool.

KYLE: Even just thinking that makes her uncool.

EDDIE: Totally.

KYLE: And she's not nearly as good looking as she probably thinks she is.

EDDIE: Yeah, like anyone cares that she has blond hair.

KYLE: Or blue eyes.

EDDIE: You couldn't pay me to have blue eyes.

KYLE: Or those eyelashes.

EDDIE: Yeah, have you seen her eyelashes?

KYLE: I'm looking at them right now.

EDDIE: Ridiculously long.

KYLE: And the way she dresses.

EDDIE: Always so perfect.

KYLE: Yeah, like even when she's messy she still looks perfect.

EDDIE: Really sad.

KYLE: Someone should tell her.

EDDIE: Yeah.

KYLE: I'm gonna go tell her that, like, we're totally on to her.

EDDIE: Or maybe I will.

KYLE: What?

EDDIE: I want to be the one to tell her that we're totally on to her.

KYLE: It's OK. I'll do it.

EDDIE: No. I will.

KYLE: I was completely not into her before you were not into her.

EDDIE: Uh unhh.

KYLE: Uh huh.

EDDIE: *(Holding up one hand, ready to play odds or evens.)* OK, odds or evens.

KYLE: *(Holding up one hand, ready to play.)* Odds.

EDDIE: One, two, three, go! *(EDDIE and KYLE both put out two fingers.)* I win! *(EDDIE turns and takes a step towards where Rachel is standing, then stops short.)* Hey, wait a second. Why is *Justin* talking to Rachel?

KYLE: He would.

EDDIE: I hate the way all the guys around here just keep feeding her ego.

KYLE: Disgusting.

EDDIE: Hey, do you see what Megan is wearing tonight?

KYLE: Pathetic.

EDDIE: Someone should tell her.

KYLE: Right?

(EDDIE and KYLE look at each other, thinking.)

- END SCENE -

ORANGE

(Scene for two people.)

(At start, BAILEY stands alone in a field or on a hilltop, watching the sunset. After a few moments, BLAIR enters and for a few more moments BOTH look at the sunset silently. They don't know each other.)

BAILEY: Nice sunset.

BLAIR: Definitely above average.

BAILEY: *(After a small pause.)* Whenever I see a sunset like this, it makes me feel all . . . orange.

BLAIR: Orange?

BAILEY: Like – warm. Like in front of a fireplace.

BLAIR: *(Still looking at the sunset.)* Huh.

BAILEY: But not just that. It makes me feel like – like also that maybe the world is really a bunch of different worlds, you know? And like they all have different colors and different feelings and that, maybe, for like that second, the world I'm in is one of the best ones. Orange.

BLAIR: Huh.

BAILEY: Why – what do you feel?

BLAIR: You mean . . ?

BAILEY: What do you feel when you look at the sunset? This sunset. Now.

BLAIR: *(After a pause.)* . . . Nothing.

BAILEY: Nothing?

BLAIR: I don't feel anything.

BAILEY: But . . . everybody does.

BLAIR: Not everybody. Some people do . . . Some people just wish they did.

BAILEY: But – I can't tell if you're joking.

BLAIR: I wouldn't. I mean I used to. Feel something. I used to come here all the time and wait for . . . wait for an orange world. And I did feel good.

BAILEY: But not any more?

BLAIR: Things happen – and sometimes you get stuck in just one world. A grey one, or a brown one, or a black one. And you can wait and wait for the orange one, but . . . *(BLAIR pauses.)* That's why I'm here today. I'm still waiting.

BAILEY: *(Earnestly.)* It's here! It's all around – right now. I can feel it.

BLAIR: *(With a slight sense of sadness.)* Yeah. I know you can . . . I gotta go.

BAILEY: Come back tomorrow.

BLAIR: I don't know.

BAILEY: Come. I'm here every day.

BLAIR: *(Smiling slightly.)* OK Sunshine. Maybe I'll see you tomorrow. *(BLAIR looks at Bailey thoughtfully for a moment.)* Later.

(BLAIR turns and starts to exit.)

BAILEY: *(To BLAIR's retreating back.)* Bye. *(BAILEY turns back toward the sunset with a slight frown. As BAILEY looks at the sunset, gradually the frown fades and is replaced by a gentle, peaceful smile. Quietly, with a sense of wonder.)* Orange.

- END SCENE -

WOODCHUCKS

(Scene for three people.)

(This scene takes place on the first day of summer camp. At start, JESS is standing center, looking around at the buildings and grounds. After a few moments, QUINN enters holding a piece of paper.)

QUINN: Hey. Are you a woodchuck?

JESS: What?

QUINN: Are you a woodchuck?

JESS: Do I look like a woodchuck?

QUINN: How should I know? This is my first summer here.

JESS: What are you talking about?

QUINN: Didn't you get an orientation sheet? It says what cabin you're in. *(QUINN shows JESS the piece of paper.)* See. I'm a woodchuck.

JESS: Oh, I didn't even look at it. *(JESS pulls out a folded up piece of paper and unfolds it.)* Ummm. Yeah, woodchuck.

QUINN: Cool. You ever gone to camp here before?

JESS: No.

QUINN: Yeah, me neither. But I heard they don't have a lot of candy, so I brought a whole backpack full, just in case.

JESS: Cool. I brought a bunch of firecrackers. Just in case.

QUINN: In case of what?

JESS: In case we need to set off some firecrackers in the middle of the night.

QUINN: Awesome!

(RORY enters.)

RORY: Hey are you guys beavers?

JESS & QUINN *(Together.)* Do we look like beavers?

RORY: How should I know? It's my first summer here. I'm actually a woodchuck, but someone said there were a bunch of beavers around.

JESS: You're a woodchuck?

RORY: Yeah.

QUINN: Us too!

RORY: Cool. *(RORY looks around a moment, hesitating.)* Don't tell anyone, but I brought my pet snake.

QUINN: Does he like candy?

RORY: He doesn't, but I do.

JESS: Firecrackers?

RORY: He doesn't, but I do. But you know what he *does* like? Hiding under the blankets in someone's bed and then scaring the life out of them!

QUINN: That sounds like a really cool snake.

RORY: Yeah, his name is Sneak. Sneak the Snake. I'll show him to you later. He's in my duffle bag.

JESS: *(To both.)* I got to tell you, I totally didn't want to come here.

QUINN: I told my mom going to summer camp was the dumbest idea ever.

(RORY nods in agreement.)

JESS: But you know, I got to say, it might actually be alright. I mean, if you get to be a woodchuck.

RORY: Yeah, cuz if you're not, what's the point?

QUINN: Maybe there's even some other decent woodchucks.

RORY: Yeah! . . . Where's the cabin, anyway?

QUINN: *(Looking at the piece of paper still in his hand.)* I think this thing has a map.

(JESS and RORY crowd around and look at the paper in QUINN's hand.)

JESS: Umm, I think it's right over there. *(JESS points.)*

RORY: No, that's the dining hall. I think it's over there. *(RORY points in a completely different direction.)*

QUINN: It doesn't matter, we'll find it. *(JESS, QUINN and RORY start to exit.)* Go woodchucks!

RORY: Yeah. Go woodchucks!

JESS: Totally. Woodchucks!

(JESS, QUINN and RORY exit.)

- END SCENE -

BREAK UP

*(Scene for one Male and one Female.
Either role can be either gender.)*

PAT: Listen, I don't think we should see each other any more.

VAL: You're breaking up with me?

PAT: Um, I guess. It's just that . . .

VAL: I knew it! I always knew you'd break up with me!

PAT: No you didn't.

VAL: I did. Right from the start. I always knew you'd break up with me.

PAT: You're being ridiculous.

VAL: No. It's true. You're just like everyone else.

PAT: No. No. It's just that . . .

VAL: You are! Sooner or later everyone always breaks up with me. They get me to like them and then they . . . You're just like Alex. Just like Chris. You're just like all of them. You were just waiting, weren't you?

PAT: That doesn't even make any sense. Why would I go out with you if . . .

VAL: *(VAL cuts PAT off.)* Because I deserve it. Because I'm not good enough. I'm never good enough.

PAT: You are! You're totally good enough.

VAL: No. No. That's the reason you're breaking up with me. Because nothing I do is ever good enough.

PAT: No! You *are* good enough. You're, you're great!

VAL: You mean it?

PAT: Yes! Yes! You're great!

VAL: You know what? That makes it even worse. That means you're just doing it to hurt me. Get away!

PAT: No, no! I would never hurt you!

VAL: Get away from me!

PAT: I . . . I love you.

VAL: *(Looking away.)* I can't even look at you.

PAT: Look at me.

VAL: No!

PAT: Look at me.

VAL: *(Looking back at Pat. Coldly.)* I would never go out with someone like you.

PAT: Please keep going out with me.

VAL: No.

PAT: Please?

VAL: You're not just going to be like Chris?

PAT: No!

VAL: Or Alex?

PAT: No!

VAL: Or any of them?

PAT: No, no, no!

VAL: You're not just going to get me to like you again and then hurt me?

PAT: No! Never! I would never do that.

VAL: Tell me again that you love me.

PAT: I love you.

VAL: OK. But this is your last chance.

PAT: OK.

VAL: Right?

PAT: I said OK!

VAL: Alright, I got to go now, but meet me here after English.

PAT: Yeah. OK. Fine. *(VAL exits. PAT looks after VAL and slowly gets a "what just happened" look.)* Huh?

- END SCENE -

LEMONADE

(Scene for two people.)

(JAMIE and DYLAN have competing lemonade stands, just a few feet apart. The lemonade stands can just be two tables or, if necessary, the stands – and their pitchers and glasses – can all be imaginary. JAMIE and DYLAN each stand behind their own table and call out to people passing by – but, at first, they don't speak directly to each other.)

JAMIE: Lemonade!

DYLAN: Lemonade!

JAMIE: Get your lemonade!

DYLAN: Ice cold lemonade!

JAMIE: *(Throwing a look at Dylan.)* Coldest lemonade on the block!

DYLAN: *(Throwing a look at Jamie.)* Coldest lemonade in town!

JAMIE: Coldest lemonade in the world!

DYLAN: Made with fresh lemons!

JAMIE: Made with fresh lemons grown in my grandmother's back yard!

DYLAN: Made with fresh lemons that didn't have bugs and roaches all over them! Fresh from the grocery store!

JAMIE: Lemonade that actually tastes good!

DYLAN: Lemonade that tastes better than those other lemonade stands!

JAMIE: Lemonade made just five minutes ago!

DYLAN: Three minutes ago!

JAMIE: One minute ago!

DYLAN: Lemonade that hasn't been made yet!

JAMIE: *(Looking at and speaking directly to Dylan.)* Ha! *(Looking back at the passersby.)* Lemonade that you don't have to wait for someone to make!

DYLAN: *(Speaking directly to Jamie.)*: You know, it wasn't even your idea to start a lemonade stand. You stole that from me.

JAMIE: Yeah, but I was the first one to actually do it.

DYLAN: By like two minutes.

JAMIE: So what? I still got here first. This is *my* corner. Go get your own corner.

DYLAN: This corner is right in front of my house.

JAMIE: Yeah? And it's right next door to *my* house. You don't own the sidewalk.

DYLAN: Well ha, ha – you haven't sold a single glass of lemonade all day.

JAMIE: Well neither have you.

DYLAN: Arrghh! I hate spending the whole day getting lemons and making lemonade and standing here in the sun and not selling anything.

JAMIE: Yeah? Well I hate it even more.

> *(JAMIE and DYLAN glare at each other angrily for several moments.)*

DYLAN: What kind of people even set up lemonade stands and then don't sell a single glass?

JAMIE: No one I want to be.

DYLAN: Me neither.

(After a moment, JAMIE gets a thoughtful look.)

JAMIE: Tell you what. If you buy a glass of lemonade from me, I'll buy one from you and then we can both quit.

DYLAN: Works for me. *(DYLAN pours a glass of lemonade and hands it to JAMIE.)* That'll be one dollar.

> *(JAMIE puts the glass on his/her table, pulls out a dollar and hands it to DYLAN. JAMIE then pours out a glass of lemonade and hands it to DYLAN.)*

JAMIE: That'll be *two* dollars. *(DYLAN gives Jamie a look.)* Just kidding.

> *(JAMIE holds out hand and gets the same dollar back from DYLAN. DYLAN then picks his/her glass of lemonade back up from his/her table and raises it in a toast.)*

DYLAN: To lemonade.

JAMIE: Lemonade.

(BOTH drink.)

- END SCENE -

PROTECTION

(Scene for two people.)

(BLAIR and CASEY are in school. They've seen each other around, but are not friends. At start, CASEY, who has just been taunted by some other kids, is angry and miserable.)

BLAIR: Why you let them do that? *(CASEY glares at BLAIR.)* Why you let them make fun of you?

CASEY: I don't *let* them.

BLAIR: Well you don't stop them.

CASEY: You get used to it.

BLAIR: Yeah - you look real used to it.

CASEY: You know, you really are . . . *(BLAIR instantly bristles and gives CASEY a look. CASEY stops short.)* You think they don't make fun of you?

BLAIR: Not to my face.

CASEY: There's no difference.

BLAIR: Yeah - there is.

CASEY: The stuff they say about you. Do you know they call you . . .

BLAIR: *(Cutting CASEY off.)* Stop! I don't want to know. That's the point.

CASEY: What point?

BLAIR: Every time they want to say something to my face but they're afraid to, I win. Every time they even *think* something, but they can't say it, they're showing me respect. I win, and they lose, a hundred times a day. And you know how that feels? It feels the exact opposite of how you feel right now.

CASEY: I can't . . . I can't be like you.

BLAIR: You don't have to.

CASEY: Then they're just gonna keep . . .

BLAIR: *(Cutting CASEY off.)* You don't have to because I like winning. Because every time I see what they do to you, I know that's what they'd do to me if they could.

CASEY: But I'm not you.

BLAIR: Doesn't matter. From now on, you'll be protected by me. And as soon as everyone knows it, no one will touch you.

CASEY: But why? We're not friends.

BLAIR: I told you. I like winning. And every day, when they want to bother me and they can't and then they want to bother you and they can't, I'll win twice.

CASEY: Who even thinks like that?

BLAIR: You saying no?

CASEY: No! *(Uncertainly. Holding out hand to shake BLAIR'S hand.)* I'm saying . . . thank you.

BLAIR: *(Ignoring CASEY'S hand. Coldly.)* That's not what this is about.

CASEY: *(Still holding out hand.)* I just want to . . .

BLAIR: *(Cutting CASEY off.)* Don't push it.

CASEY: I won't. *(BLAIR turns and starts to walk away. CASEY calls after BLAIR. Louder.)* I won't! *(BLAIR exits. CASEY heaves a big sigh of relief, then speaks quietly, in the direction BLAIR exited.)* Thank you.

- END SCENE -

UNDERSTANDING

(Scene for two people.)

(In the following scene, RORY is a person. BONKERS is a dog. Throughout the scene, although RORY talks directly to BONKERS, RORY does not expect BONKERS to truly listen or understand – which means that, generally, RORY is really just talking to RORY. BONKERS, being a dog, is also really just talking to BONKERS. As the scene begins, BONKERS races in, stops, pants, looks around, smells the air, pants some more, and looks back. RORY enters.)

RORY: I am so happy to be out of that house.

BONKERS: *(Eagerly looking around.)* I am so glad to be out of that house!

RORY: Everyone was really getting on my nerves.

BONKERS: *(Looking at Rory.)* Walkies!

RORY: You know what I mean? Sometimes you just need to get out.

BONKERS: *(Running ahead of Rory, then running back.)* I could go for walkies all day long.

RORY: Just leave everyone behind.

BONKERS: Walkies all day, every day.

RORY: And did you hear what Mom said to me? That really stinks.

> *(BONKERS bends down and smells some object on the ground.)*

BONKERS: Wow. This really stinks. *(BONKERS continues smelling the object on the ground.)*

RORY: What difference does it make if I clean my room every day or not? It's just gonna get messy again.

BONKERS: *(BONKERS looks up at Rory. Happy and excited.)* Really, really stinks!

RORY: *(Patting BONKERS on head.)* You know, sometimes talking to you is the only thing that keeps me going. I know you really listen.

BONKERS: *(Suddenly seeing a squirrel in a tree.)* Hey you lousy squirrel! Come down here! Come down here!

RORY: Bonkers, no!

BONKERS: *(To squirrel.)* Wait til I catch you! You've got to come out of that tree sometime!

RORY: Bonkers, come! *(RORY walks away from the squirrel. BONKERS follows after RORY.)* Now what were we talking about?

BONKERS: Dumb squirrel. I wish I could climb trees . . .

RORY: You're so lucky you're a dog. You can do whatever you want.

BONKERS: . . . but I can't climb trees. I can't even go outside and pee whenever I want.

RORY: I wish I was a dog.

BONKERS: I wish I was a person.

RORY: *(Looking at BONKERS.)* But at least I have you.

BONKERS: *(Looking at RORY.)* But at least I have you.

RORY: You know what? You're the only one who really understands me.

BONKERS: I wish I could understand even one thing you say.

(BONKERS and RORY look at each other fondly.)

RORY & BONKERS: *(Simultaneously.)* I love you.

(RORY turns and starts walking.)

RORY: C'mon!

(BONKERS runs after RORY. BOTH exit.)

- END SCENE -

START

(Scene for one Male and one Female.)

(TOM and KATE sit in silence, a couple of feet apart, thinking their own thoughts. THEY remain silent for several moments.)

KATE: You ever think about things?

TOM: Course I do. Who do you think I am?

KATE: I mean big things.

TOM: Like what?

KATE: Like why are we here?

TOM: *(Shrugs.)* Nothing better to do.

KATE: No, I mean why are we all here? For what?

TOM: *(Thinks a moment.)* I think it's like Mr. Kerwin says in science. Survival. We're here to eat and fight and win and . . . *(TOM looks KATE directly in the eye.)* . . . you know.

KATE: *(Looking away.)* He was talking about animals.

TOM: We're all animals.

KATE: I don't believe that.

TOM: Then why do *you* think we're here?

KATE: I think it's more like to . . . to help each other survive.

(TOM snorts derisively.)

TOM: You don't know anything.

KATE: I know as much as you do. Anyhow, nothing else makes sense.

TOM: Why not?

KATE: OK, then why are there so many of us? If we're only here to eat and win, then in the end there should just be one person left. And that's the winner.

TOM: Maybe there will be.

KATE: And you think that's winning?

TOM: Well, it's not losing.

KATE: What about . . . (KATE hesitates.)

TOM: What?

KATE: What about loneliness?

TOM: What about it?

KATE: It's like being hungry. The last person in the world would maybe have all the food there is, but he'd be lonely.

TOM: Maybe.

KATE: So he'd be hungry.

TOM: I don't know.

KATE: Don't you ever feel lonely?

TOM: (Slightly angrily.) I'm a winner.

KATE: But don't you?

(KATE puts her hand on TOM's.)

TOM: *(More angrily.)* I'll *never* be hungry.

> *(TOM and KATE look each other directly in the eye for a moment.)*

KATE: Yeah. I can see that.

> *(KATE takes her hand off of TOM's.)*

TOM: *(Looking away.)* Good.

> *(There is an awkward moment of silence.)*

KATE & TOM: *(Simultaneously.)* Listen, I . . . *(BOTH stop, waiting for the other to finish speaking.)*

KATE: You first.

TOM: No, you first.

KATE: I should go now.

TOM: Yeah. You should go.

KATE: OK.

> *(KATE stands up. KATE pauses, looking at TOM, who looks at the floor. KATE turns to go.)*

TOM: *(Hesitantly.)* If you want . . . I mean . . . I don't care, but if you want, I could walk with you for a little. If you want.

> *(KATE looks at Tom, thinking.)*

KATE: OK. Maybe for a little.

> *(TOM stands up.)*

TOM: OK. *(Indicating a direction.)* That way?

KATE: Yeah. Let's start that way.

(TOM and KATE exit.)

- END SCENE -

LOST

(Scene for three people.)

(TERRY, JAMIE and PJ are hiking in the woods.)

TERRY: Where are we?

JAMIE: I don't know.

PJ: I think we're lost.

TERRY: We're definitely lost.

JAMIE: I don't know if we're lost. Maybe we just don't know where we are.

PJ: That's the same thing. Being lost and not knowing where you are are the same thing.

JAMIE: You think you're so smart.

PJ: I know I am.

JAMIE: Then why don't you tell us where we are?

TERRY: Enough! We need to figure out how to get back to the trail.

JAMIE: Yeah, let's just go to back to the trail . . . Where's the trail?

PJ: That's what we're trying to figure out.

TERRY: What if we just walked back exactly the way we came?

JAMIE: Yeah.

PJ: OK. *(ALL THREE look around, thinking.)* Which way did we come?

JAMIE: *(Pointing.)* I totally remember passing that tree. *(Pointing in a different direction.)* Unless it was that tree.

PJ: *(To Jamie.)* I'm never going hiking with you again. *(To both.)* Does anyone have a compass?

TERRY: Why would anyone bring a compass?

PJ: *(Pointedly.)* Because we're going hiking. In the woods.

TERRY: Well, I didn't bring one.

JAMIE: I didn't bring one.

PJ: You guys are unbelievable.

JAMIE: Well, you didn't think to bring one either.

PJ: I did so think to bring one. I just figured everyone else was already bringingone.

TERRY: Anyway, what difference would it make? We don't know if the trail is north, south, east or west of here.

JAMIE: Well, it's definitely one of those.

PJ: *(To Jamie.)* Just be quiet.

> *(JAMIE turns away from PJ and stands with back to PJ, Terry and the audience.)*

TERRY: OK, why don't we start to figure out what we're gonna do if we have to spend the night here.

PJ: We should collect some firewood.

TERRY: And find some water.

PJ: And maybe, like, make a tent out of some pine branches and stuff.

JAMIE: *(Still with back to PJ, Terry and the audience.)* Or we could just walk to the road that's like a hundred yards that way.

PJ: *(Dismissively.)* What are talking about?

> *(JAMIE turns around and we see that she/he is looking at a cell phone.)*

JAMIE: I went on Google Maps. There's a road right over there.

TERRY: Alright Jamie! Let's go!

> *(ALL THREE start to walk towards where Jamie pointed.)*

JAMIE: *(To PJ.)* I told you there's a difference between being lost and not knowing where you are.

PJ: You think you're so smart.

JAMIE: I know I am.

> *(ALL THREE exit.)*

- END SCENE -

STARS

(Scene for one Female, one Male.)

> *(JORDAN, who is always nervous, awkward and shy around people, has just stepped outside from a party. HE is standing alone, looking at the stars. After several moments, SKYLER steps outside from the party.)*

SKYLER: Hey.

JORDAN: *(Looking at Skyler. Nervously.)* Oh . . . I . . . Hey.

SKYLER: What are you doing out here?

JORDAN: I, um, I – just getting some air.

SKYLER: *(Looking up at the stars, then back at Jordan.)* It's nice out.

JORDAN: Out here? I – yes.

SKYLER: *(Indicating the party.)* It's a good party.

JORDAN: *(Looking back towards the party. Weakly.)* Fun!

> *(JORDAN looks up at the stars. After a moment SKYLER looks up too.)*

SKYLER: Remember how we used to go out and look at the stars in your back yard in, like, second grade?

JORDAN: *(Relaxing slightly.)* You said you were going to be an astronaut.

SKYLER: And you said you'd watch me on TV.

JORDAN: Yeah.

SKYLER: You know Cara really likes you.

JORDAN: *(Suddenly nervous again.)* No.

SKYLER: She told me.

JORDAN: *(Turning away.)* No. No.

SKYLER: *(Gently.)* You should go talk to her.

JORDAN: I . . . I can't.

SKYLER: *(Placing a hand on JORDAN's shoulder.)* You can.

JORDAN: *(Shrinking away from SKYLER's touch.)* No. No. No . . . I
wouldn't know what to say.

SKYLER: Sure you would. Once you start. *(JORDAN continues
looking at the ground.)* You could practice first. Pretend I'm Cara.
(JORDAN continues looking at the ground.) Just say hi. Pretend
I'm Cara and say hi.

> *(JORDAN looks at Skyler nervously. Small pause.)*

JORDAN: Hi . . . Cara.

SKYLER: Hi Jordan.

JORDAN: I . . . I . . .

SKYLER: You can do it.

JORDAN: It's a . . . It's a good party. Isn't it?

SKYLER: *(Encouragingly.)* It's a really good party.

JORDAN: And I . . . I . . . I've been waiting a really long time for
someone to notice me.

SKYLER: I don't know if . . .

JORDAN: *(Cutting SKYLER off.)* And, and I was wondering
if maybe sometime you wanted to come over to my

JORDAN *(Cont.)*: house . . . Cara . . . and we could go in my back yard and maybe look at the stars and . . .

SKYLER: *(Gently.)* Jordan.

JORDAN: And we could talk about when you become an astronaut and maybe . . .

SKYLER: Jordan.

JORDAN: And maybe you could . . . we could . . . I wouldn't . . .

SKYLER: *(Putting her hand on JORDAN's shoulder.)* Jordan.

JORDAN: *(Pulling away. Scared and angry.)* Don't look at me!

SKYLER: Jordan, I came out here because . . .

JORDAN: *(Cutting SKYLER off.)* I don't care! I don't care why! I just . . .

> *(JORDAN stops short, staring at the ground and shifting from foot to foot. SKYLER looks at JORDAN sympathetically for several moments.)*

SKYLER: I should go inside.

JORDAN: *(Still staring at the ground.)* . . . Yes.

SKYLER: See you inside? *(JORDAN doesn't answer.)* OK.

> *(SKYLER exits in the same direction she entered. After SKYLER has left, JORDAN looks over in the direction where she exited, then glances up at the stars, then down at the ground again.)*

JORDAN: *(Quietly, almost in a whisper.)* Come back . . . Come back . . . Come back.

- *END SCENE* -

BORED

(Scene for two people.)

> *(PAT and AJ are lying on their backs, looking at the sky.)*

PAT: I'm bored.

AJ: SO bored.

PAT: I think if I was any border my head would explode.

AJ: I think mine just did. *(AJ sits up and pantomimes head exploding.)* Arggghhh. POOOM!

PAT: *(Sitting up.)* Why did we come here anyway?

AJ: To meet up with Chris and those guys.

PAT: That was like an hour ago.

AJ: More.

PAT: So where are they? *(AJ shrugs.)* We should go do something else.

AJ: But what?

> *(AJ and PAT stare ahead, thinking, for several moments.)*

PAT: We could go to your house.

AJ: Nah. I'm sick of my house . . . We could go to your house.

PAT: Nah. Too boring.

AJ: Yeah.

PAT: *(Standing up.)* We should go to McDonald's!

AJ: *(Standing up.)* Yeah!

PAT: Do you have any money?

AJ: Nah.

PAT: Me neither.

> *(AJ and PAT sit back down and are silent for several moments.)*

AJ: *(Laying back and looking at the sky.)* You ever look at clouds?

PAT: Not really.

> *(PAT lays back and looks at the sky.)*

AJ: Yeah, me neither.

PAT: Stars sometimes.

AJ: Yeah, stars are cool.

PAT: None out right now.

AJ: Too early.

PAT: Yeah. Maybe tonight.

AJ: Yeah, maybe tonight.

PAT: I am so bored.

AJ: REALLY bored.

PAT: Completely, absolutely, totally bored.

AJ: We should go do something.

PAT: Yeah. We really should.

AJ: Yeah.

> (PAT and AJ continue to lie on their backs, not moving.)

- END SCENE -

THE DOG

(Scene for two people.)

(REESE is sitting alone on the floor, looking depressed. SAGE enters.)

SAGE: What's wrong?

REESE: Nothing.

SAGE: *(Pressing the matter.)* What.

REESE: *(Angrily.)* Nothing!

SAGE: That's it? That's all you have to say?

REESE: That, and go away.

SAGE: Listen, I know.

REESE: You don't know anything.

SAGE: Sarah told me your parents are splitting up.

REESE: Sarah should learn to mind her own business.

SAGE: You want to talk?

REESE: Does it sound like I want to talk?

SAGE: Why do you always have to make it so hard?

REESE: Make what so hard?

SAGE: Make it so hard for people to be nice to you?

REESE: Is that what you're being? Nice?

SAGE: Trying. *(REESE shrugs. SAGE sits on the floor, next to Reese.)* Look, when my parents split up, no one wanted to talk about it. Not even them. I didn't have anybody to talk to.

REESE: It's not fair! I didn't do anything!

SAGE: Doesn't matter.

REESE: *(Angrily.)* It matters to me!

SAGE: No, I mean - it's not about doing something. You didn't do anything to make it happen and you couldn't have done anything to make it not happen. It's just . . . them.

REESE: You think so?

SAGE: I know so. It's like if you fight with your sister and the dog goes and hides. He thinks he did something, but he didn't. He didn't start the fight and nothing he does can stop the fight.

REESE: You're saying I'm the dog? *(Angrily.)* You're saying I'm the dog!?!

SAGE: *(Thinks a moment, then gently.)* . . . You're the dog . . . We're both the dog. You don't get to pick who you are. You only get to be who you are.

REESE: Is that supposed to make me feel better?

SAGE: I don't know. Do you feel better?

REESE: A little.

SAGE: Yeah.

REESE: *(Standing up.)* You want to go get some fries?

SAGE: *(Standing up.)* I don't have any money.

REESE: It's OK. Since my parents aren't talking, they both gave me my allowance this week.

(SAGE and REESE start to exit.)

SAGE: Silver lining, right?

REESE: Yeah, silver lining.

(Exit.)

- END SCENE -

ANSWERS

(Scene for two people.)

(NICKY and TAYLOR are in a classroom taking a test. Their desks are next to each other.)

TAYLOR: *(Whispering.)* NICKY! *(NICKY doesn't respond. Louder.)* NICKY!! *(NICKY bends over his/her test sheet to cover the answers. Louder.)* NICKY!!!

NICKY: *(Annoyed. Whispering.)* What?

TAYLOR: What's the answer to number seven?

NICKY: How should I know?

TAYLOR: I saw you write something down.

NICKY: That was for number six.

TAYLOR: Oh . . . What's the answer to number six?

NICKY: Are you serious?

TAYLOR: *(Slightly embarrassed.)* I know.

NICKY: We studied this together.

TAYLOR: I know.

NICKY: Last night.

TAYLOR: I *know* . . . Is it fourteen?

NICKY: What!?!

TAYLOR: The answer to number six. Is it fourteen?

NICKY: It's India.

TAYLOR: The country?

NICKY: Are you even reading the questions? Seriously.

TAYLOR: Why do you have to be that way? We can't all be geniuses. You know, some people are good at taking tests and some people . . .

(NICKY cuts TAYLOR off.)

NICKY: And some people are good at cheating off of people who are good at taking tests.

TAYLOR: You know what? Forget it. I don't need your answers. They're probably wrong anyway.

NICKY: (Pleadingly.) Taylor. (TAYLOR ignores NICKY.) Taylor – come on.

TAYLOR: Forget it. I'm gonna get an A without you.

NICKY: Taylor, you know you can't.

TAYLOR: I so much can. (TAYLOR bends over the test sheet and starts filling in the answers – saying each answer out loud, just loud enough for NICKY to hear – as NICKY watches.) Number one is George Washington. Number two is – sulfuric acid. Number three is a unicorn. Number four is 85 miles an hour . . .

(NICKY interrupts.)

NICKY: You know this is a geography test, right?

TAYLOR: Darn it! Darn it! I'll never get this right!

NICKY: You can definitely do it. If you think about it, you can come up with the right answer.

TAYLOR: You think so?

NICKY: I know so. Just think.

(TAYLOR stares at the test paper, thinking hard. After a few moments, TAYLOR smiles.)

TAYLOR: I have it! I have the answer!

NICKY: You do?

TAYLOR: *(Raising hand. Eagerly.)* Mr. Shapiro! Mr. Shapiro! *(TAYLOR pauses a moment as Mr. Shapiro answers.)* Yes, I know it's the middle of a test. *(Mr. Shapiro answers again.)* Yes, I know. But I just got a text from my mom. I have to go home right away and take care of my baby sister. *(Mr. Shapiro answers again.)* Yes, I know it's unusual, but she has a real problem and this is the only answer she could think of. *(Mr. Shapiro answers again.)* Thank you! Thank you! *(TAYLOR stands up.)* Yes, I'll be happy to take a different make-up test tomorrow. Gotta go! *(TAYLOR stands up, gives a quick, secret smile to NICKY and exits.)*

NICKY: *(Watching TAYLOR exit, to self)* Hunh. He/She really did come up with the answer. *(NICKY goes back to taking test.)*

- END SCENE -

ANXIETY

(Scene for two Females and one Male OR two Males and one Female.)

NOTE: If RILEY is male, ALEX and SYDNEY are female.
If RILEY is female, ALEX and SYDNEY are male.

> *(SYDNEY has a crush on RILEY. SYDNEY has asked ALEX to write a poem to help him/her let RILEY know. ALEX has just written that poem for SYDNEY. Unfortunately, ALEX also has a secret crush on RILEY.*
>
> *At start, ALEX and SYDNEY stand together on one side of the performance area. They BOTH look at a sheet of paper torn out of a notebook. As SYDNEY – who is holding the sheet – reads, SYDNEY's lips move silently. RILEY stands away from them on the opposite side of the performance area next to a table, chair or other surface. RILEY is unaware of them and playing with a cellphone.)*

SYDNEY: *(Finishing reading.)* This is great. This is perfect!

ALEX: Thanks.

SYDNEY: How do you write this stuff? This is exactly how I feel.

ALEX: I know . . . I mean, I figured that was probably how you feel. Felt. Feel.

SYDNEY: Thanks. I owe you.

ALEX: It's OK.

SYDNEY: Look, he's/she's right there. I'm gonna give it to him/her right now.

ALEX: Yeah . . . Good luck.

SYDNEY: Thanks. *(SYDNEY goes over to RILEY. Shyly and hesitantly.)* Hey, I, um . . . *(RILEY puts away the cellphone.)* . . . I wrote something . . . Something that I wrote for you.

RILEY: Really?

SYDNEY: Yeah. It's right here.

> *(SYDNEY hands RILEY the sheet of paper.)*

RILEY: Wow. No one ever . . . Wow . . . It's a poem?

> *(Unnoticed by RILEY, ALEX takes a step or two closer, watching and listening.)*

SYDNEY: Yeah. I wrote it for you.

RILEY: Should I read it?

SYDNEY: Yeah. It's really good.

> *(Unseen by RILEY, SYDNEY briefly turns and gives ALEX a quick smile and a thumbs-up. ALEX smiles uncomfortably and gives a quick nod.)*

RILEY: *(Clears throat and reads.)* "Anxiety."

SYDNEY: That's the title.

RILEY: I know. It's really good. *(Clears throat and continues reading. As RILEY reads, ALEX watches RILEY intensely.)*
"I worry about a lot of things
Like global warming
And tooth decay
And math tests –
Because I'm not very good at math
But most of all
I worry that another day will go by
That you don't notice me"
(To SYDNEY.) Aww. *(SYDNEY smiles. ALEX gets a sad look and continues to stare at RILEY. RILEY continues reading.)*

RILEY *(Cont.)*: "Romeo and Juliet
  They noticed each other right away
  Like the grass notices the rain
            *(ALEX, staring at RILEY, recites the next three lines
            silently as RILEY reads them out loud.)*
  But I can walk right by you in the hall
  And you can't see me
  And I worry that I might be invisible
            *(ALEX stops reciting silently and continues to stare
            sadly at RILEY.)*
  Or that your world is so far away from mine
  That you don't even know I'm out there"
            (To SYDNEY.)
  You really wrote this?

SYDNEY: I wrote it for you.
            *(ALEX starts to say something, but stops before
            making a sound, then continues to look pained and sad.
            SYDNEY leans over the piece of paper in RILEY's
            hands and reads.)*
  "Once I worried for two whole weeks
  When I lost one of my gloves
  But even that glove couldn't feel as lost as me
  Every time I see you in English
  Or social studies
  Or the bus"

            *(SYDNEY looks up and smiles at RILEY. RILEY
            smiles back and starts to read.)*

RILEY: "So instead of worrying
  I decided to write this poem"
            (To SYDNEY.)
  Aww.
            (Continuing to read.)
  "And I hope that you don't see the words
  Or the paper
  Or the way my heart is pounding
  When you open it and read it.
  I hope that all you see is me
  Because I worry about a lot of things"

69

(ALEX, still staring sadly at RILEY, recites the last three lines of the poem silently – as RILEY reads them out loud – then continues to watch SYDNEY and RILEY.)

RILEY *(Cont.)*: "But most of all
  I worry that another day will go by
  That you don't notice me"
        (To SYDNEY.)
  It's really good.

SYDNEY: Right?

RILEY: *(Placing the poem on a nearby table or chair.)* But you know, you didn't need to write a poem. I liked you even before that.

SYDNEY: You did?!?

RILEY: Yeah.

SYDNEY: Really?

RILEY: Yeah.

SYDNEY: *(After a pause.)* . . . Are you going to the cafeteria?

RILEY: Yeah. Come with?

SYDNEY: Yeah!

(SYDNEY and RILEY cross the playing area together, right in front of ALEX, then exit. ALEX goes over to the poem, picks it up and looks at it. ALEX looks sadly towards where SYDNEY and RILEY exited, then crumples up the poem and stands, sadly and silently.)

- END SCENE -

LUCKY BREAK

(Scene for two people.)

(CASEY is lying in bed with a newly broken leg. CHRIS enters.)

CHRIS: Hey.

CASEY: *(Depressed.)* Hey.

CHRIS: I heard about your leg.

CASEY: Yeah.

CHRIS: Bummer.

CASEY: Yeah.

CHRIS: Does it hurt?

CASEY: Yeah.

CHRIS: A lot?

CASEY: Yeah.

CHRIS: A real lot?

CHRIS: *(Getting annoyed.)* Yes.

CASEY: Bummer. *(There is an awkward silence for several moments.)* Could you, like, hear it when it broke? Did it go, like, KKRKKKRRSSHHHH?

CHRIS: Kind of.

CASEY: What did it sound like? I mean exactly.

CHRIS: *(Annoyed.)* Like. My leg. Was breaking.

CASEY: Right. Right. So do you, um, get to miss school and stuff?

CHRIS: *(Perking up a little.)* Actually, yeah.

CASEY: That's awesome.

CHRIS: Plus I can do whatever I want all day.

CASEY: Really?

CHRIS: Yup. After today, my mom won't even be here.

CASEY: Sooo . . . TV?

CHRIS: Yup.

CASEY: Video games?

CHRIS: Yup.

CASEY: *Ice cream?*

CHRIS: There's like four gallons in the refrigerator right now.

CASEY: Wow. But . . . it really hurts, right?

CHRIS: Not so much when I'm watching TV or eating ice cream.

CASEY: Right. Right. That makes sense . . . You think I could maybe come over tomorrow after school and help you with your, like, recovery and ice cream and stuff?

CHRIS: Yeah. Definitely.

CASEY: That'd be awesome.

CHRIS: Yeah. *(Indicating the cast on the broken leg.)* You want to sign it?

CASEY: Really?

CHRIS: Yeah. Go ahead.

CASEY: *(Pulling out a pen and writing on the cast.)* "To the luckiest kid I know. Signed Casey." *(CASEY finishes and stands up.)*

CHRIS: So, see you tomorrow?

CASEY: Definitely. See you tomorrow.

> *(CASEY exits. CHRIS settles back in bed and puts his/her hands behind head with a big sigh of contentment.)*

CHRIS: *(Loudly.)* Hey Mom! Do you think you can bring me some ice cream?

> *(CHRIS smiles.)*

- END SCENE -

TRAP

(Scene for two people.)

(TRACY and WHITNEY are siblings. WHITNEY is sitting, reading a book. TRACY enters carrying a dead mouse in a mousetrap.)

TRACY: What did you do? What did you do?

WHITNEY: Nothing.

TRACY: What do you call this?

WHITNEY: What?

TRACY: *(TRACY angrily throws the mouse, still in the trap, at WHITNEY's feet.)* This!

WHITNEY: What. It's nothing.

TRACY: You killed it!

WHITNEY: So what?

TRACY: You killed it!

WHITNEY: It's a mouse.

TRACY: And you killed it! You had no right!

WHITNEY: What are you talking about? Of course I had a right. It was a mouse. They're vermin.

TRACY: It was alive.

WHITNEY: It was disgusting.

TRACY: You're disgusting. Maybe someone should crush *you*.

WHITNEY: Look, there are a million mice out there. There's probably like 1,000 just in this house. Go fall in love with one of them and leave me alone.

TRACY: I can hear them crying.

WHITNEY: Who?

TRACY: The mice. All the mice. I can hear them crying.

WHITNEY: You know there's something seriously wrong with you, right? Anyway, I didn't kill it. I just set a trap and it walked into it.

TRACY: Yeah? Well, be careful. Maybe one of these days someone will set a trap for you.

WHITNEY: Who - you?

TRACY: I know where you go. I know what you think. And I know what will hurt you.

WHITNEY: Go back to Crazytown. I heard there's a rat there that's crying for you.

TRACY: *(Picking up the mouse, which is still in the trap.)* You'll be sorry. You're not the only one that knows how to set traps.

(TRACY starts to exit.)

WHITNEY: Look, I'm sorry. *(TRACY continues to walk away. WHITNEY calls uneasily after Tracy.)* It was just a mouse. *(TRACY exits. Louder.)* It was just a mouse!

- END SCENE -

ART

(Scene for two people.)

(DREW and BLAIR enter, each carrying a camera or using the cameras on their phones. DREW enters enthusiastically, slightly ahead of BLAIR.)

DREW: Come on, we have to do sixteen outdoor photos each and then we're done.

BLAIR: Ugh, I hate this. This is so boring.

DREW: It's easy! *(Looking up.)* Look – that building has some pretty cool graffiti, right? *(DREW takes a photo of the graffiti.)*

BLAIR: Fine.

> *(BLAIR takes a photo of the graffiti. DREW looks at BLAIR disapprovingly for a moment.)*

DREW: That cloud's pretty cool. *(DREW takes a photo of the cloud.)*

BLAIR: I guess. *(BLAIR takes a photo of the cloud.)*

DREW: No – you can't just keep taking the same pictures I take.

BLAIR: Who says?

DREW: You're supposed to, like, be relying on your own judgment.

BLAIR: Well, I judge that you've got good taste.

DREW: That's my cloud.

BLAIR: You can't just call a cloud.

DREW: Yes you can. I saw it first.

BLAIR: Nobody owns the clouds.

DREW: No, but I own the *picture* of the cloud.

BLAIR: Great. You own your picture, I'll own mine.

DREW: No – it doesn't work that way. We can't just show up with all pictures of the same things. We have to have our own different pictures.

BLAIR: He won't even notice.

DREW: Of course he'll notice! Both our last names start with S. Our pictures will be right next to each other on the wall.

BLAIR: I hate this class.

DREW: Then why did you take it?

BLAIR: Umm. Because you *asked* me to.

DREW: I only asked you 'cuz I thought I'd be fun.

BLAIR: It's not.

DREW: It *is*! And it's easy! Look - anything can be art. You just have to . . . to look for it. Graffiti can be art. Clouds can be art. Garbage can be art!

BLAIR: In this class it can.

DREW: I'm serious. Look at that garbage can. The way all the paper and bottles and everything is just pouring out of the top and piling up all around it – it's like a fountain. You take a picture, you call it "Fountain," and it's art.

BLAIR: *(Getting a little interested.)* You think so?

DREW: I know it!

BLAIR: *(Sullenly.)* Go ahead. I won't copy you.

DREW: No – it's for you.

BLAIR: *(Genuinely pleased.)* Really?

DREW: Yeah! *(BLAIR picks up the camera, looks at the garbage can through it, squints, circles around the can, squats, stands up, etc., looking for the perfect angle, then takes the photo.)* Lemme see.

(BLAIR shows DREW the photo.)

BLAIR: Art?

DREW: Art.

(BLAIR smiles.)

BLAIR: OK, but you can't keep calling everything first. You can't call the whole world.

DREW: Look, I'll make you a deal. I'll split it with you.

BLAIR: What?

DREW: We'll split the world. I'll photograph my half, you photograph your half.

BLAIR: OK - I call North America and South America. You can have the rest.

DREW: Why are you being such a pain?

BLAIR: I just want to make sure there's something good in my half.

DREW: Alright, tell you what. You take everything from the waist down, I'll take the waist up. That graffiti and that cloud is above the waist.

BLAIR: The head.

DREW: What?

BLAIR: I own everything to the top of my head.

DREW: Done. *(Suddenly looking up.)* Oh! Look at that pigeon. *(DREW takes a picture.)*

BLAIR: *(Looking down.)* Gum wrapper! *(BLAIR takes a picture.)*

> *(DREW and BLAIR start to exit, still looking around and taking photographs – DREW looking up, BLAIR looking down.)*

DREW: That shadow on the building! *(DREW takes a picture.)*

BLAIR: Cigarette butt in the gutter! *(BLAIR takes a picture.)*

DREW: Are you just gonna take pictures of garbage all day?

BLAIR: Didn't anyone ever tell you? Garbage can be art.

(DREW and BLAIR exit.)

- END SCENE -

WIN

(Scene for three people.)

(VAL, AVERY and SAGE are on the same soccer team. They are in the middle of a game, discussing the next play. VAL is the captain.)

VAL: OK - now if we score this last goal, we win the game.

AVERY: I don't know if I agree with that statement.

VAL: What are you talking about?

SAGE: Avery is right. You need to define your terms.

VAL: Winning. It's the opposite of losing.

AVERY: But is it really winning if, in the process, we take away the other team's dignity? That doesn't sound like a situation where the general concept of winning is either created or enhanced.

SAGE: Yeah - you just said that winning is the opposite of losing. But if one side wins and the other side loses, then they cancel each other out. Altogether, no one wins.

VAL: *(Irritated.)* *We* will win! If we do this play the way I'm saying, *we* will win and they will lose.

AVERY: I don't know if I'm comfortable with that. Some people have fragile egos.

SAGE: Or demanding parents.

AVERY: Or a pathological need to win. No one *needs* to win.

VAL: *(More irritated.)* I do. We do. I'm the captain of this team and we have not won a single game all season. We need to win. This game. Today.

SAGE: I feel that there are a lot of issues coming up right now for the middle of a game. Maybe we should forfeit and go discuss them.

VAL: No! I'm the captain! We're not forfeiting. I'm the captain!

AVERY: You need to stop saying that.

VAL: I AM the captain.

AVERY: Welllll . . .

VAL: You voted for me!

SAGE: We really only voted for you because you wanted to be captain so bad.

AVERY: And we didn't care.

SAGE: Yeah.

AVERY: Still don't.

SAGE: Not even a little.

VAL: But . . .

AVERY: *(To SAGE.)* You feel like going for a walk or something?

SAGE: I'm down with that.

VAL: But we can win this! We can win this!

AVERY: Winning is when you're happy with yourself. I'm happy. *(To SAGE.)* You happy?

SAGE: I'm happy.

AVERY: Go team! *(AVERY and SAGE start to exit. After several steps, SAGE turns around. To VAL.)* You coming?

(VAL stares at them in disbelief.)

VAL: *(After a moment. Resigned.)* Fine. *(VAL walks over to SAGE and AVERY. ALL THREE start to exit.)* But this is the last time. *(ALL THREE continue walking.)* I mean it. The really, really last time.

(ALL THREE exit.)

- END SCENE -

GONE

(Scene for two people.)

(JAMIE and DEVON are cousins. They are at a reception for a relative who has passed away. They've just stepped away from the reception into another room. As JAMIE and DEVON enter, JAMIE glances back momentarily into the room they've just left.)

JAMIE: I feel bad about Aunt Julie.

DEVON: Yeah.

JAMIE: No, not 'cuz she's dead. And not because you're supposed to feel bad about someone at their funeral. More because . . .

DEVON: What?

JAMIE: I don't know, because . . .

DEVON: What?

JAMIE: Because I never really liked her.

DEVON: Seriously?

JAMIE: I mean, she was always really nice to me. And she wasn't a bad person. I mean, not that - she was a good person. A totally good person. She just always . . . She just always bugged the hell out of me.

DEVON: You too?

JAMIE: *(Surprised.)*: What?

DEVON: Whenever my mother told me she was coming over, I always used to go hide in my room.

JAMIE: Me too!

DEVON: My dad always had to go upstairs and make me come down.

JAMIE: All those questions. Like she was trying to psycho-analyze me or something.

DEVON: She used to drive me crazy with that. Like, three times in a row, "Do you want to tell me more about that? Do you want to tell me more about that?"

JAMIE: Yes! Just stop already. Yes, what I said is what I really meant. Can we talk about something normal now?

DEVON: One time I actually said to her, "Can we just talk about the weather?" And she couldn't do it. She totally couldn't do it.

JAMIE: I know . . . But I still feel bad.

DEVON: Yeah. I mean now that she's – gone.

JAMIE: But the thing is, I . . .

(JAMIE hesitates.)

DEVON: What?

JAMIE: I don't know. I just worry that . . .

DEVON: What?

JAMIE: That I might actually miss her.

DEVON: *(Sadly.)* Yeah . . . I know. *(After a moment, DEVON gets a sly smile.)* Do you want to tell me more about that?

JAMIE: *(Smiles.)* Don't even try it.

DEVON: C'mon, let's go back in.

(JAMIE and DEVON exit in the same direction from which they entered.)

- END SCENE -

KNOWLEDGE

(Scene for two people.)

(JESS and REESE are sitting next to each other on a school bus.)

JESS: Where's this field trip going again?

REESE: Museum of Natural History.

JESS: They got dinosaurs there?

REESE: Course they got dinosaurs there.

JESS: You know they're not real right?

REESE: What?

JESS: Dinosaurs. They were made up in like 1946 to trick the Nazis.

REESE: Trick them into doing what?

JESS: I dunno. Believe in dinosaurs I guess.

REESE: That's the dumbest thing I ever heard.

JESS: You don't know nothing. It's completely true. It was on the Internet.

REESE: Really?

JESS: Yup. Swear on my mother.

REESE: *(Convinced.)* Huh. I read on the Internet that the entire country isn't actually controlled by the president anymore. It's

REESE *(Cont.)*: secretly run by like three people inside the Washington Monument. And one of them is Albert Einstein.

JESS: Don't be dense. Albert Einstein is dead.

REESE: That's how much you know. Just before he died, they put his head in this jar full of goo. He runs the country from a jar.

JESS: That's not true.

REESE: It's totally true. I read it on the Internet. Go look it up.

JESS: *(Convinced.)* Huh.

REESE: Imagine if there was like some guy who was just making stuff up and like he found some way to put it on the Internet.

JESS: That would be insane!

REESE: Yeah, like anything. Two plus two equals seven. Or everyone over 6 feet tall is an alien.

JESS: That could never happen. Albert Einstein would go crazy on that guy. You're talking ridiculous.

REESE: I'm just saying it would be funny.

JESS: Yeah, it'd be pretty funny. *(Pulling out a bag of M&Ms.)* Hey – do you want a M&M?

REESE: Yeah. Thanks.

>   *(REESE holds out a hand and JESS pours some
>   M&Ms into REESE's palm.)*

JESS: Don't eat the green ones. They cause cancer.

REESE: Internet?

JESS: Yeah.

(REESE picks out two M&Ms and drops them back in the bag.)

REESE: Good to know.

(JESS and REESE sit and eat their M&Ms, thinking.)

- END SCENE -

LAST WORDS

(Scene for two people.)

(LANE and RILEY are old friends. LANE enters, followed by RILEY several feet behind.)

LANE: *(Stopping and looking back. Frustrated.)* Come *on*. Why are you so slow?

RILEY: What's the difference?

LANE: Why can't you just walk the same speed as me?

RILEY: We're only going to the store. What difference does it make what time we get there?

LANE: It's just that you have to stop and look at *everything*. We walk down this same street every day. Nothing has changed since yesterday.

RILEY: So what? We're not doing anything. We don't have to be anywhere. We're just . . . going to the store 'cuz we couldn't think of anything else to do.

LANE: It's just that everything always takes forever with you.

RILEY: Why are you being such a pain?

LANE: I'm just sick of it.

RILEY: Sick of what?

LANE: Sick of dealing with it.

RILEY: With *it*? You mean with me?

LANE: Fine. Yes. With you.

RILEY: You're sick of dealing with me?

LANE: You're just – I don't know. You're just not any fun anymore.

RILEY: Because I walk slow?

LANE: No. Yes. No. It's just everything.

RILEY: *(Angrily.)* Like what?

LANE: Like your hamsters. I'm so sick of hearing about them. Why do you have to tell me every day about your hamsters?

RILEY: I thought you liked the hamsters.

LANE: I used to. Like three years ago. But it's every day. I don't *care* how much food they ate this morning. I don't care what they did when the cat came into the room. I just don't care.

RILEY: Well you think I care about playing ping pong in your basement every day? It's fun for like five minutes.

LANE: So don't play it.

RILEY: But that's all you ever want to do.

LANE: Then don't play with *me*.

RILEY: What?

LANE: I . . .

RILEY: You don't want to hang out with me anymore?

LANE: I didn't say . . .

RILEY: That's exactly what you said.

LANE: Then yes. I don't want to hang out with you anymore. You're boring.

RILEY: I can't believe I ever liked hanging out with you!

LANE: Well now you don't have to.

RILEY: Good.

LANE: Good.

RILEY: And don't sit next to me anymore in school.

LANE: Don't worry about it. I won't.

RILEY: Or at lunch. I'm gonna sit with my real friends.

LANE: You're pathetic.

RILEY: You are.

LANE: You are.

RILEY: I'm done.

> *(RILEY turns and walks away in the direction they entered from.)*

LANE: *(Calling after Riley.)* Hey - don't walk too slow or you'll never get back to your hamsters!

> *(RILEY exits. LANE turns and angrily continues walking towards the store. Exit.)*

- END SCENE -

SUMMER

(Scene for two people.)

(MORGAN and JOJO are sitting next to each other in class.)

MORGAN: Can you see it?

JOJO: See what?

MORGAN: The clock. Can you see the clock?

JOJO: *(Twisting to see the clock.)* Yeah.

MORGAN: What's it say?

JOJO: Two more minutes.

MORGAN: Two more minutes of school til the beginning of summer.

JOJO: Right? It's amazing!

MORGAN: *(Glumly.)* It's forever.

(JOJO twists around again to look at the clock.)

JOJO: Ninety seconds.

MORGAN: Aghh! I'll never make it!

JOJO: Hold on! We're almost there.

MORGAN: It's too much! It's too much!

JOJO: Show a little courage.

MORGAN: All those days! Those hours. All that math. And history. And science. Ugh – the science, dude, the *science*!

(*JOJO twists around again to look at the clock.*)

JOJO: Sixty seconds.

MORGAN: I'm standing up.

JOJO: Don't do it.

MORGAN: I'm standing up.

JOJO: Don't do it! They'll make you stay after.

MORGAN: They wouldn't.

JOJO: They would.

MORGAN: They wouldn't!

JOJO: And then summer will never come.

MORGAN: (*Putting hands to head.*) Aghhh!

(*Suddenly, MORGAN and JOJO look up simultaneously as they hear the bell.*)

JOJO: What was that?

MORGAN: The bell!

JOJO: The bell?

MORGAN: It was the bell!

JOJO: (*Standing up.*) That's it! It's summer! Summer is here!

MORGAN: (*Standing up, then looking up.*) Thank you, thank you, thank you!

JOJO: So what should we do now? *(JOJO and MORGAN stare blankly at each other for several moments. Finally, MORGAN shrugs and BOTH sit back down.)* Hunh.

(JOJO and MORGAN stare blankly at each other for several more moments.)

- END SCENE -

SIBLINGS

(Scene for three Females OR three Males.)

> *(ALEX, BRETT AND CHRIS are siblings. ALEX is the oldest. BRETT is in the middle. CHRIS is the youngest. They are either all three girls or all three boys – be sure to choose the word "sisters" or "brothers" in the script accordingly. At start, ALL THREE are standing several feet apart from each other, facing the audience.)*

ALEX: Sisters/Brothers.

BRETT: Sisters/Brothers.

CHRIS: Sisters/Brothers.

ALEX: Can't live with them.

BRETT: Can't make them move away.

CHRIS: *(Looking at Alex.)* You can't even make them move one foot away. Like if they're sitting too close to you on the sofa.

ALEX: *(Looking at Chris.)* Or burping.

BRETT: *(Looking at Brett.)* Or talking on the phone. Forever.

> *(ALEX, BRETT and CHRIS glare at each other for a moment.)*

CHRIS: Anyway.

BRETT: Anyway.

ALEX: Anyway. Having a little brother/sister is like having a cold. Sometimes you can forget you have it, but it just keeps coming back.

BRETT: *(Looking at Chris.)*: And when it does come back, it's eating the Doritos that you specifically said you were saving for when your favorite show comes on.

CHRIS: *(To Brett.)* You can't call dibs on food.

BRETT: Yes you can.

ALEX: No you can't.

CHRIS: No you can't.

> *(ALEX, BRETT and CHRIS glare at each other for a moment.)*

BRETT: Anyway.

CHRIS: Anyway.

ALEX: Anyway. Maybe the worst part of having sisters/brothers is if you have to share a room.

BRETT: Sharing a room is the worst.

CHRIS: It's like being punished for something you didn't do.

ALEX: Every. Single. Day.

BRETT: And the punishment doesn't stop even when you leave the house. *(Looking at Alex.)* Because having an older sibling means that all your new clothes are things that somebody else already wore.

CHRIS: *(Looking at Chris.)* That two people already wore.

ALEX: *(To Brett.)* Why do you have to be such a baby about it?

BRETT: Why do you have to draw on your clothes with Magic Marker?

ALEX: Because it looks cool.

BRETT: It does not.

ALEX: Does so.

CHRIS: Does not.

ALEX: Does so.

BRETT: Then draw on your own clothes.

CHRIS: Yeah.

ALEX: Those *are* my own clothes. When I draw on them.

> *(ALEX, BRETT and CHRIS glare at each other for a moment.)*

BRETT: Anyway.

CHRIS: Anyway.

ALEX: Anyway. Having two sisters/brothers means that you never get to be alone.

BRETT: But also that you never *have* to be alone.

CHRIS: And that even if sometimes they're not on your side – when you need them, they're always on your side.

ALEX: And everyone knows it.

BRETT: *Everyone* knows it.

CHRIS: *(Looking at Alex.)* So even if they hog the sofa.

ALEX: *(Looking at Brett.)* Or burp.

BRETT: *(Looking at Chris.)* Or talk on the phone all day, all night, every day until you want to scream.

CHRIS: It just might be worth it.

ALEX: Possibly.

BRETT: Maybe . . .

CHRIS: If he'd/she'd just stop drawing on the clothes.

BRETT: Hogging the Doritos.

ALEX: Walking on my side of the room.

ALL THREE: *(Yelling. Angrily.)* Just stop!

> *(ALEX, BRETT and CHRIS glare at each other for a moment.)*

CHRIS: Anyway.

ALEX: Anyway.

BRETT: Anyway.

CHRIS: *(Rolling eyes.)* Sisters/Brothers.

- END SCENE -

WEIRD

(Scene for two people.)

> *(WHITNEY sits alone on the floor, drawing in a notebook. CASEY enters.)*

CASEY: Oh sorry. I didn't know anyone was in here.

WHITNEY: Maybe no one is in here.

CASEY: I can see you.

WHITNEY: But can you see yourself?

CASEY: What is that supposed to mean?

WHITNEY: What do you think it means?

CASEY: I don't actually care.

WHITNEY: Then go.

> *(WHITNEY goes back to drawing. CASEY stands and watches for a moment, thinking.)*

CASEY: Why do you always have to be so weird?

WHITNEY: *(Continuing to draw.)* Who says I'm weird?

CASEY: Pretty much everyone.

WHITNEY: Maybe that's not a bad thing.

CASEY: It's probably not a good thing. I mean, if you want friends or whatever.

WHITNEY: *(Stopping drawing and looking up.)* Yeah. I know . . . People kind of scare me.

CASEY: How come?

WHITNEY: I don't know.

CASEY: They're not that scary.

WHITNEY: For you.

> *(WHITNEY returns to drawing. CASEY thinks a moment.)*

CASEY: Maybe you're not actually scared. Maybe you just think you're scared.

WHITNEY: *(Looking up.)* There's no difference between thinking you're scared and being scared.

CASEY: I guess. Maybe you could start with one person.

WHITNEY: Like who?

CASEY: I don't know. *(WHITNEY goes back to drawing. CASEY watches for several moments.)* What are you drawing?

WHITNEY: I don't know. It's either a dinosaur or some kind of alien.

CASEY: Maybe an alien dinosaur.

> *(WHITNEY smiles momentarily.)*

WHITNEY: Yeah, maybe.

CASEY: I used to draw dinosaurs a lot.

WHITNEY: Yeah?

CASEY: Yeah.

> *(WHITNEY tears a piece of paper out of the notebook and pushes it towards CASEY.)*

WHITNEY: Let's see.

CASEY: Yeah?

WHITNEY: *(Going back to drawing.)* If you want.

CASEY: OK. *(CASEY sits down, pulls out a pen or pencil and starts to draw. WHITNEY stops drawing and watches. After a moment, CASEY looks up.)* It's a brontosaurus.

WHITNEY: I don't think they had big fangs.

CASEY: They do when I draw them.

WHITNEY: . . . Sometimes I make mine all orange and pink. Weird, right?

CASEY: Maybe not so weird. For all anyone knows, maybe they *were* orange and pink.

WHITNEY: Orange and pink with big fangs.

CASEY: *Really* big fangs.

> *(CASEY goes back to drawing. WHITNEY watches a moment, then goes back to drawing.)*

WHITNEY: Yeah, fangs are cool.

> *(CASEY and WHITNEY continue drawing.)*

- END SCENE -

CANADA

(Scene for two people.)

(JAMIE and DALE are friends. At start, DALE stands alone. JAMIE enters.)

JAMIE: I just thought you should know I'm leaving.

DALE: Where are you going?

JAMIE: That's not important.

DALE: What is important?

JAMIE: Why I'm leaving.

DALE: Why *are* you leaving?

JAMIE: Because no one understands me. So I'm going to Canada.

DALE: I thought that wasn't important.

JAMIE: Well it's important to me. How could that not be important?

DALE: You just said it wasn't important.

JAMIE: See that's what I mean. No one understands anything I say.

DALE: What you said was where you're going isn't important.

JAMIE: But someone who understood me would know what I *meant*.

DALE: What did you mean?

JAMIE: I meant . . . I don't know . . . I meant, act like you care that I'm leaving.

DALE: Well, no one understands me either.

JAMIE: Don't even try that. Everyone understands you.

DALE: No they don't.

JAMIE: I do.

DALE: No you don't. If you understood me, you'd know that I wanted you to agree with me when I said that no one understands me.

JAMIE: See. That's why I'm going to Canada. Nobody understands anybody here. Maybe you should go somewhere too.

DALE: But what if it's no different there?

JAMIE: Where?

DALE: Anywhere. Everywhere. What if no matter where you go, it's all just people who don't really understand each other?

JAMIE: What?!?

DALE: That no one totally understands anyone else anywhere.

JAMIE: But then . . . Then what . . ?

DALE: Then nothing. Then is now.

JAMIE: But . . . then there would be no point in going to Canada.

DALE: Yeah.

JAMIE: Or anywhere.

DALE: Yeah. So you might as well just stay here and try to get someone to understand you. A little.

JAMIE: You think that's possible?

DALE: Maybe. A little. I think if people really try, maybe Canada can be anywhere.

JAMIE: Really?

DALE: Yeah. Like – like your own personal Canada.

JAMIE: Wow. *(JAMIE thinks a moment.)* I guess *real* Canada is probably super cold right now anyway.

DALE: Probably.

JAMIE: . . . And I don't even know how to get there.

DALE: So stay. That's what you wanted me say in the first place, right?

JAMIE: Yeah.

DALE: Stay.

- END SCENE -

THE END

(Scene for three people.)

(As the scene begins, SANDY is in the middle of telling a story to friends JESS and QUINN.)

SANDY: So then she said, "No!" And I said, "Yes!" And she said, "I don't believe it!" And I said, "Well, you better believe it, because . . ."

JESS: *(Cutting SANDY off.)* Guys. Guys!

SANDY: Wait. I'm just getting to the good part.

JESS: Where are we?

QUINN: What do you mean? We're in the . . . *(Suddenly stopping and looking around, confused.)* We're in . . . Where are we?

JESS: *(Looking around.)* I don't really see *anything*.

SANDY: It's kind of like fog, but without the fog.

QUINN: Or nighttime, but it's light.

JESS: But . . .

SANDY: Yeah . . .

JESS: I mean, how did we get here?

QUINN: Well, I mean, I thought we were . . . I thought we were at the park.

SANDY: We were walking across the park.

JESS: On the way to soccer.

QUINN: And then I heard this noise.

SANDY: A really loud noise.

JESS: *(To QUINN.)* And you said RUN!

QUINN: And we went . . . I think we went . . .

SANDY: We definitely did.

JESS: We went into the trees.

SANDY: And I hit my shoulder on a branch.

JESS: Something hit my knee.

QUINN: And then I turned around and . . .

SANDY: And . . .

JESS: We all turned around.

SANDY: My shoulder was really hurting.

QUINN: And . . .

JESS: And . . .

SANDY: And . . .

QUINN: And then we were here.

JESS: But where are we?

QUINN: And how did we . . . ?

> *(ALL THREE look around, then back at each other.)*

SANDY: *(After a moment. Touching shoulder.)* My shoulder doesn't hurt any more.

JESS: Neither does my knee.

SANDY: I don't really feel *anything*.

QUINN: You don't think we're . . .

JESS: What.

QUINN: That something happened – like an explosion or something – and now we're . . .

SANDY: No!

JESS: No. We couldn't . . .

SANDY: We couldn't be.

JESS: No.

QUINN: But if we're not, then . . .

JESS: We should just wait. Wait and see. Maybe someone will come.

SANDY: Anyone.

JESS: If we wait.

SANDY: We should wait.

JESS: Wait and see.

QUINN: OK, then let's vote. Everyone in favor of waiting. *(ALL THREE raise their hands.)* So we'll wait. *(ALL THREE sit down, facing out, leaning their backs against each other.)* We'll wait and see . . . *(ALL THREE look around uneasily.)* We'll wait.

- END SCENE -

NOTES

DOUGLAS M. PARKER is an award-winning author, playwright and lyricist. His works include two books of original monologues – *Contemporary Monologues for Young Actors* and *Contemporary Monologues for Young Actors 2*. His theatrical works include the musical, *Life on the Mississippi*, based on Mark Twain's classic autobiographical coming-of-age tale; *BLUE: The Life and Music of Bessie Smith*, based on the rise and fall of the great American blues singer; *Thicker Than Water*, a drama based on the Andrea Yates tragedy; *Declarations*, a Young Audience historical drama drawn from the letters of John and Abigail Adams; and *The Private History of a Campaign That Failed*, a Young Audience comedy based on Mark Twain's true, humorous memoire of his time as a lieutenant in the Confederacy's least accomplished, most forgotten regiment. A graduate of Brown University and a member of the Dramatists Guild, he lives in New York City and can be reached at MonologueFrog@gmail.com.

Made in the USA
Monee, IL
17 December 2019